HAL•LEONARD

WEDDING ESSENTIALS
INCLUDES REFERENCE CD

LOVE SONGS FOR WEDDINGS

T0101567

ISBN 978-1-4234-8863-7

HAL•LEONARD® CORPORATION

7777 W. BLUEMOUND RD. P.O. BOX 13819 MILWAUKEE, WI 53213

Visit Hal Leonard Online at
www.halleonard.com

GROW OLD WITH ME

Words and Music by
JOHN LENNON

Tenderly

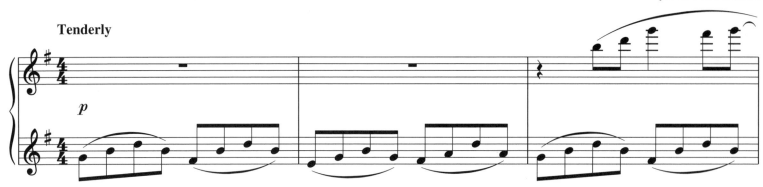

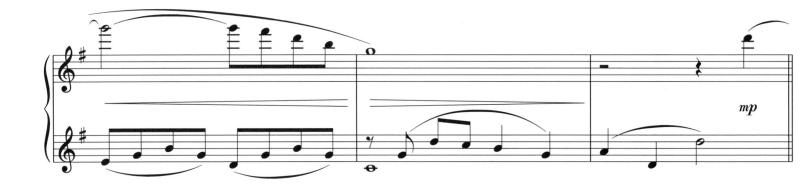

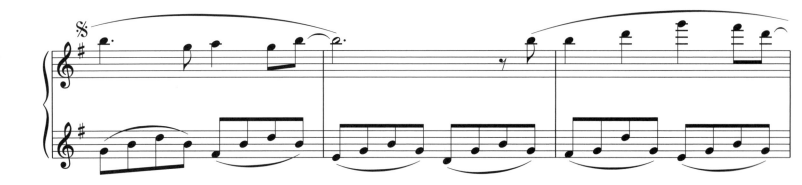

To Coda ⊕

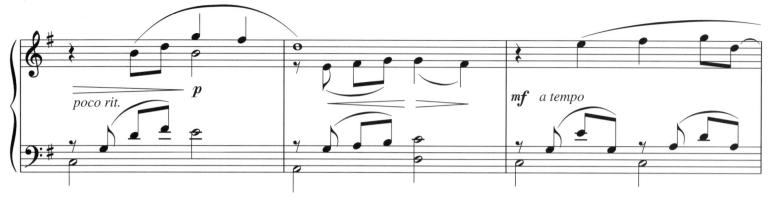

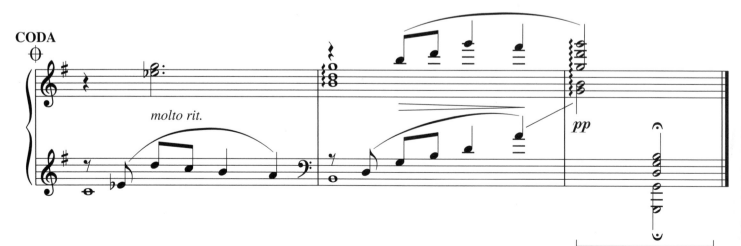

IF

Words and Music by
DAVID GATES

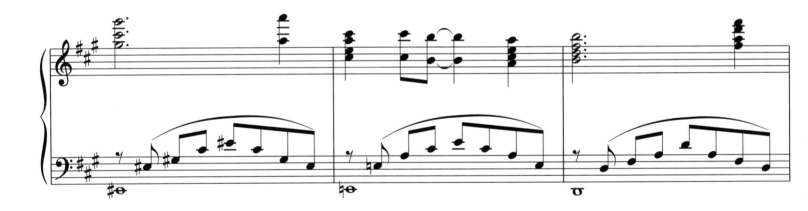

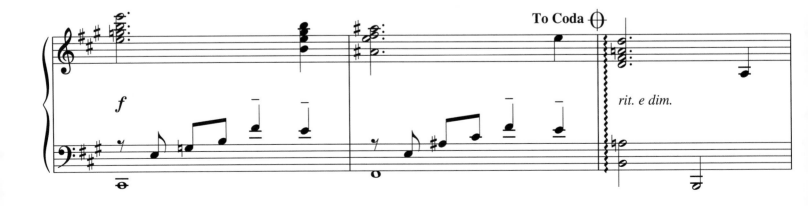

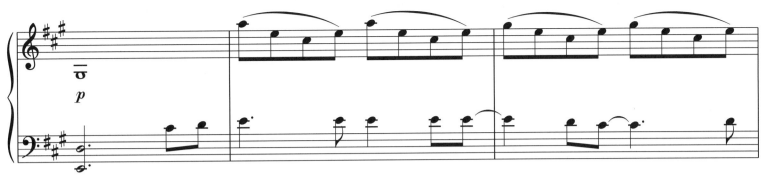

D.S. al Coda

CODA

HERE, THERE AND EVERYWHERE

Words and Music by JOHN LENNON
and PAUL McCARTNEY

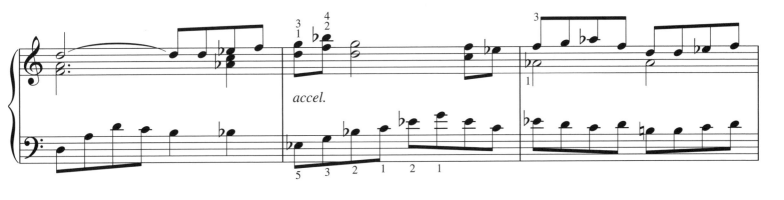

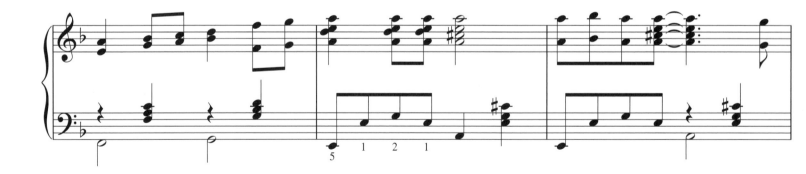

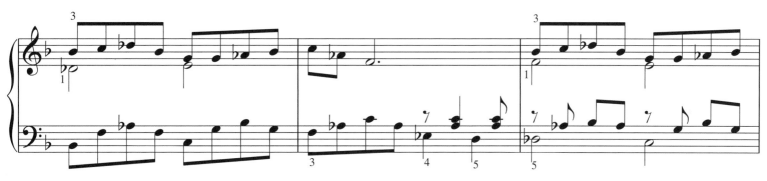

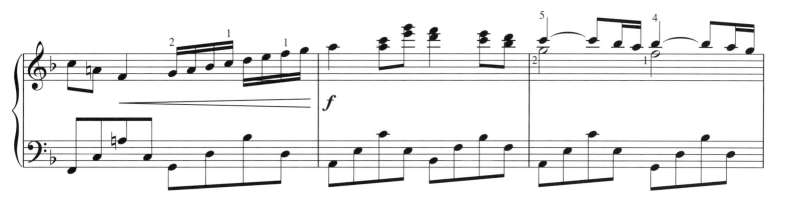

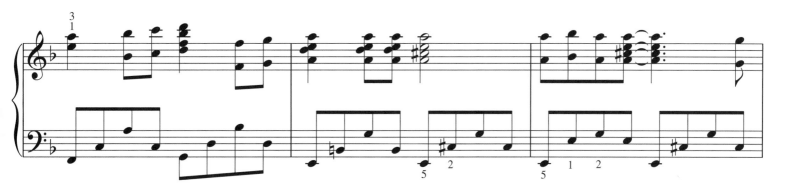

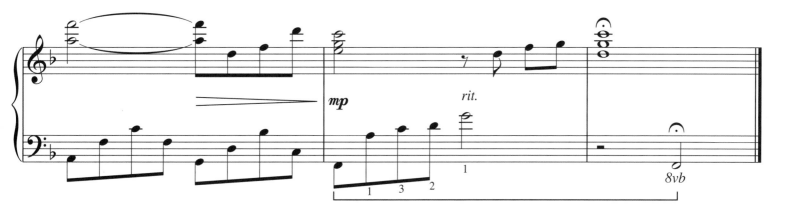

LONGER

Words and Music by
DAN FOGELBERG

Moderately

13

PART OF MY HEART

By JIM BRICKMAN

Moderately fast

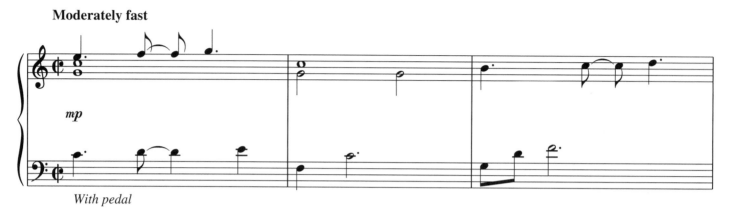

mp

With pedal

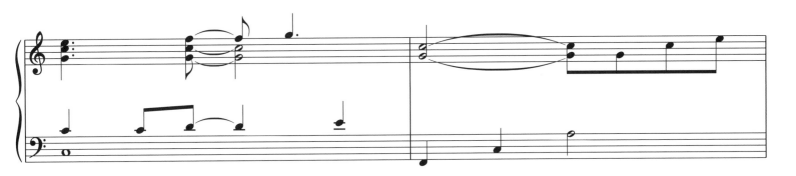

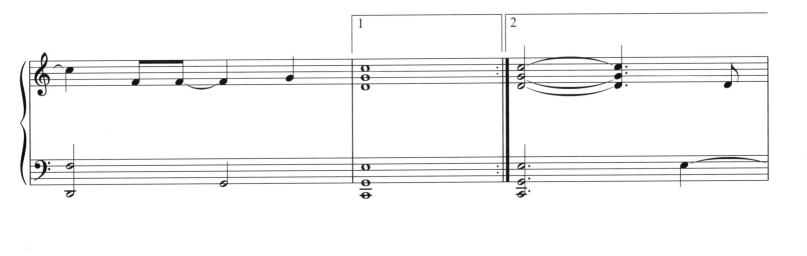

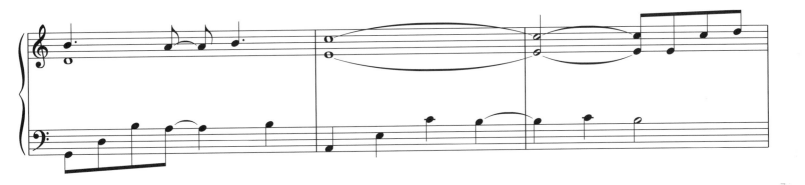

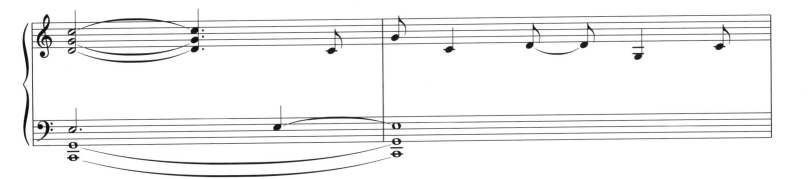

VALENTINE

Words and Music by JACK KUGELL
and JIM BRICKMAN

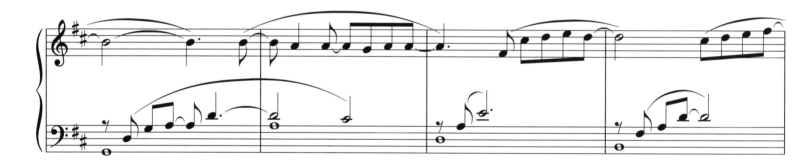

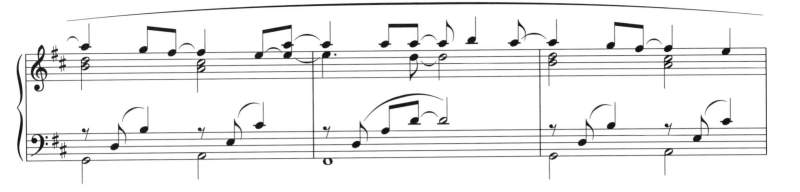

To Coda ⊕

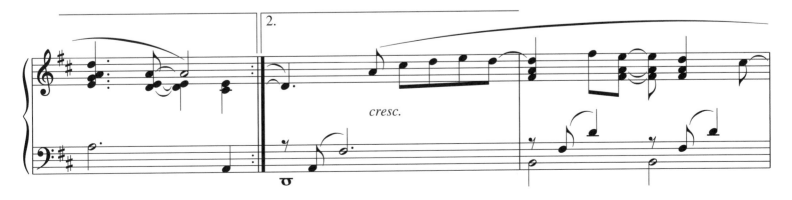

D.S. al Coda

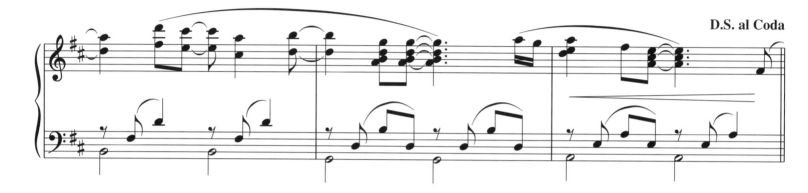

CODA

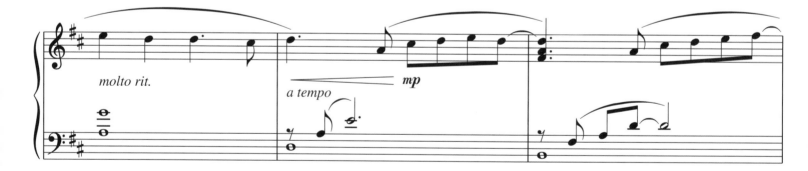

YOU RAISE ME UP

Words and Music by BRENDAN GRAHAM
and ROLF LOVLAND

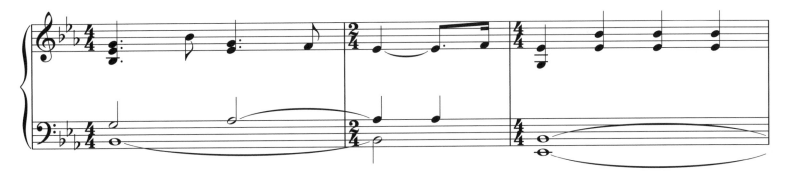

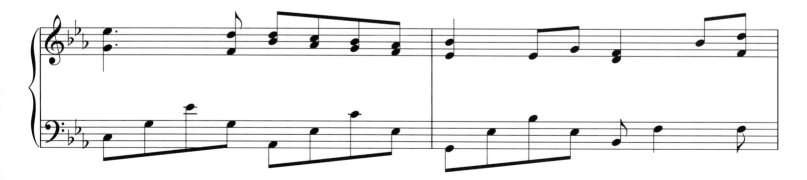

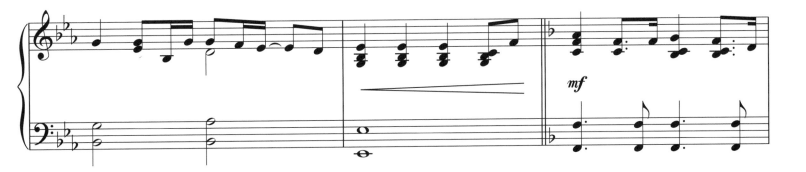

WE'VE ONLY JUST BEGUN

Words and Music by ROGER NICHOLS
and PAUL WILLIAMS

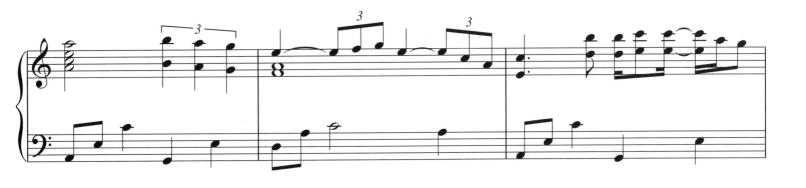

THE WEDDING SONG

By KENNY G
and WALTER AFANASIEFF

Tenderly, somewhat freely

With pedal

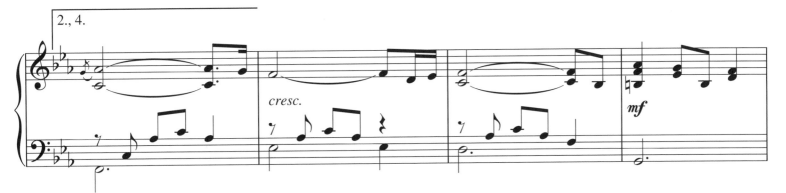

YOU AND I

Words and Music by
STEVIE WONDER

Slowly, with feeling

mp

With pedal

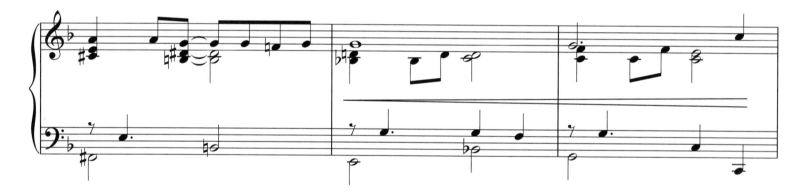

mf

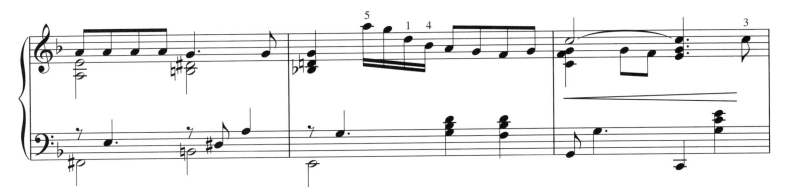

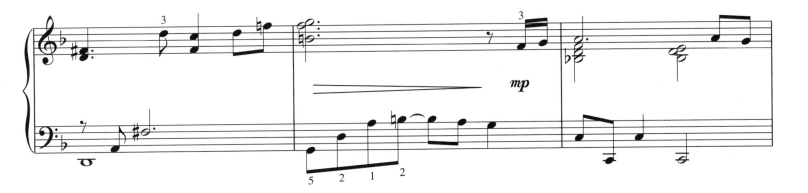

HAL•LEONARD
WEDDING ESSENTIALS

INCLUDES REFERENCE CD

Christian Wedding Favorites
Answered Prayer • God Causes All Things to Grow • God Knew That I Needed You • Household of Faith • I Will Be Here • If You Could See What I See • Love Will Be Our Home • Seekers of Your Heart • This Day • 'Til the End of Time.
00311941 P/V/G... $16.99

Contemporary Wedding Ballads
Beautiful in My Eyes • Bless the Broken Road • Endless Love • (Everything I Do) I Do It for You • From This Moment On • Have I Told You Lately • Here and Now • Love of a Lifetime • More Than Words • When You Say You Love Me.
00311942 P/V/G... $16.99

Love Songs for Weddings
Grow Old with Me • Here, There and Everywhere • If • Longer • Part of My Heart • Valentine • We've Only Just Begun • The Wedding Song • You and I • You Raise Me Up.
00311943 Piano Solo... $16.99

Service Music for Weddings
Processionals, Recessionals, Lighting of the Unity Candle
Allegro maestoso • Amazing Grace • Ave Maria • Canon in D • Jesu, Joy of Man's Desiring • Jupiter (Chorale Theme) • O Perfect Love • Ode to Joy • Rondeau • Trumpet Voluntary.
00311944 Piano Solo... $14.99

Wedding Guitar Solos
All I Ask of You • Gabriel's Oboe • Grow Old with Me • Hallelujah • Here, There and Everywhere • More Than Words • Sunrise, Sunset • Wedding Song (There Is Love) • When I Fall in Love • You Raise Me Up.
00701335 Guitar Solo... $16.99

Wedding Vocal Solos
Grow Old with Me • I Swear • In My Life • Longer • The Promise (I'll Never Say Goodbye) • Someone Like You • Sunrise, Sunset • Till There Was You • Time After Time • We've Only Just Begun.
00311945 High Voice.. $16.99
00311946 Low Voice... $16.99

Worship for Weddings
Be Unto Your Name • Broken and Beautiful • Center • He Is Here • Here and Now • Holy Ground • How Beautiful • Listen to Our Hearts • Today (As for Me and My House).
00311949 P/V/G... $16.99

For More Information, See Your Local Music Dealer, Or Write To:

HAL•LEONARD®
CORPORATION
7777 W. Bluemound Rd. P.O. Box 13819 Milwaukee, WI 53213

www.halleonard.com

Prices, content, and availability subject to change without notice.